AROUND
MALVERN
IN OLD PHOTOGRAPHS

THE WYCHE PASS c. 1912.

AROUND
MALVERN
IN OLD PHOTOGRAPHS

COLLECTED BY
KEITH SMITH

ALAN SUTTON
1989

Alan Sutton Publishing
Gloucester

First published 1989

British Library Cataloguing in Publication Data

Around Malvern in old photographs
1. Hereford and Worcester. Malvern, history
I. Smith, Keith 1942–
942.4'47

ISBN 0-86299-587-6

Typesetting and origination by
Alan Sutton Publishing
Printed in Great Britain
by Dotesios Printers Limited

CONTENTS

WE HAVE ARRIVED HERE → THE TOP OF THE MALVERN HILLS

← THE TOPOSCOPE

Published by Tilley and Son, Ledbury. Copyright.

TEA HOUSE

INTRODUCTION

This collection of photographs spans a period of over one hundred years, and reflects the subjects of interest to both professional and amateur photographers over that period. Many of the views come from public collections, and have not previously been reproduced. Some are from various family albums and have not been seen outside family circles before. Others are postcards from the heyday of the postcard era during the early years of the century. All of these photographs help to illustrate the nature of the Malverns and the people who have lived and worked in the area over the years.

Those who have long associations with the Malverns and the surrounding villages will, I trust, find their memories rekindled. Relative newcomers who, like me, have made their home in the area will, I hope, find a fascination in the past which is still reflected wherever one turns in the present. Visitors will also, hopefully, find the contents of more than just casual interest.

No records of individual photographers represented here appear to still exist, and little or no research has yet occurred relating to Malvern photographers. Michael Hallett's useful research in local directories and newspapers for the Royal Photographic Society Historical Group has produced a list of Worcestershire and Herefordshire professional photographers. Unfortunately this list does not include the prolific semi-professional and amateur chroniclers of the Malvern scene such as Clem Walton. It is to be hoped that the contents of this book will generate more interest in this most important area of historical record.

One of the saddest parts of compiling this book was the number of fascinating photographs which could not be positively identified. If you take photographs of local events or interesting buildings – please record the date, place and people concerned for future book compilers.

Streets and Buildings – The Malverns

ALTHOUGH ON A POSTCARD dated 1905, this photograph of Church Street must have been taken in the 1880s or earlier. It is the earliest known photograph of the premises of J.G. Lear & Sons, seen on the extreme right.

NOTTS THE GROCERS AND TEA DEALERS in Church Street was established in the early 1850s. This photograph of the shop, which has since been rebuilt, was taken c. 1900.

Church Street, Malvern

CHURCH STREET, C. 1904. Compare this with today's busy scene.

A CARRIAGE FOR HIRE below Belle Vue Terrace around 1900.

A LOCAL OFFICER of the constabulary, c. 1900, outside Alfred Mander's Belle Vue Pharmacy on Belle Vue Terrace. The adjoining apartments were also owned by Alfred Mander.

RED LION BANK and St Ann's Road around 1900. The single-storey building left of centre has now disappeared. The Temperance Hotel existed until at least the 1940s.

TWO POLICE OFFICERS posing in the Worcester Road, c. 1900. The Unicorn Inn is on the left.

A VIEW OF AROUND 1910 of Belle Vue Terrace. In the foreground is Edwin Trigg's cab and carriage office (now a record shop).

A VIEW OF GREAT MALVERN, c. 1908, showing the varying types of Victorian architecture.

A VIEW OF MALVERN from the Imperial Hotel, pre-1914.

A VIEW OF THE TOP OF CHURCH STREET, c. 1900. Malvern Central Supply was J.H. Jones' provision stores. Both buildings in this photograph are now shoe shops.

THE PROMENADE, Worcester Road, around 1906.

A NINETEENTH-CENTURY VIEW of Belle Vue Terrace, with Henry Guy the booksellers, stationers and printers in the middle. The business later moved to Church Street.

ROSE BANK, WELLS ROAD, in 1959, shortly before demolition. The Regency house was a gift to the town by Mr Dyson Perrins in 1918.

THE PROMENADE GARDENS were privately owned and now belong to the Abbey Hotel. This pre-1914 view shows Cox & Painter (now Warwick House) on the left and Rose Bank on the right.

A PRINT OF 1863 showing Lansdown Crescent. Built during the 1850s, the buildings on the right were demolished to make way for the new hospital around 1911.

THE ABBEY GATEWAY, c. 1900, with Cridlan & Walker the butchers on the left.

THE OTHER SIDE of the Abbey Gateway around 1900.

THE ABBEY GATEWAY AND HOTEL just after the turn of the century.

THE ABBEY GATEWAY in 1956, then still open to traffic – but only at 4 mph.

A PRE-FIRST WORLD WAR VIEW of Belle Vue Terrace, with the Mount Pleasant on the extreme left and the old vicarage down the slope on the right.

THE MOUNT PLEASANT HOTEL and the top of Bell Vue Terrace, c. 1910.

GRAHAM ROAD around 1912, facing towards Church Street.

GRAHAM ROAD facing towards the Worcester Road, c. 1912.

STOKES & HALL, Edith Walk, prior to demolition in 1980. The firm had a long history, under various names, as builders, plumbers, etc.

UPPER CHASE ROAD, Barnards Green, in 1911. The shop at the end has recently closed.

THE MOTOR HOUSE at Davenham, Graham Road, home of C.W. Dyson Perrins, 1911.

THIS IS BELIEVED TO BE A FÊTE at Davenham during the early years of the century.

A PRE-FIRST WORLD WAR VIEW of Priory Gardens showing their popularity then.

PRIORY GARDENS, MALVERN.   *No. 1.*

BELOW THE TERRACE in the Priory Gardens during the 1920s.

A VIEW OF THE IMPERIAL HOTEL in 1861. Designed by E.W. Elmslie, it was sold to Malvern Girls' College in 1919.

THE RAILWAY HOTEL, Malvern Link, 1861. Converted to a school in 1873 and demolished in 1968.

AVENUE ROAD, c. 1912. The lamps on the right (since removed) marked the entrance to the Imperial Hotel.

AVENUE ROAD in 1913 from near Barnards Green.

PRIORY CHURCH around 1912. The church was bought from King Henry VIII at the Dissolution of the monasteries for £20!

ST MATTHIAS AT THE LINK, originally built in 1846, rebuilt in 1881 and seen here c. 1912.

Malvern Link Common.

A VIEW OF LINK TOP with Newtown Road on the left in the early 1920s.

THE PENTECOSTAL TABERNACLE, on the corner of Somers Road, Malvern Link, c. 1928. It has since been rebuilt.

TRINITY CHURCH in 1853 in splendid isolation.

COWLEIGH CHURCH AND NATIONAL SCHOOLS, St Peters Road, seen here before the First World War. The school building was gutted by fire in September 1989.

GREAT MALVERN from the Link Common, taken before 1914.

MALVERN LINK COMMON, c. 1910.

PICKERSLEIGH ROAD, Malvern Link, from Link Lodge on the left to Link End on the right. Taken in 1912.

PICKERSLEIGH HOUSE, MALVERN

PICKERSLEIGH COURT (or House as in this postcard) dates from the fifteenth century.

CHARLES RUSSELL, a journeyman carpenter, and his wife outside Edith Cottage, Moorlands Road, just after the turn of the century.

TOM RUSSELL AND HIS FAMILY outside The Hermitage, Pickersleigh Road, around 1900. He was a gardener and obviously a good cabbage grower!

WORCESTER ROAD, Malvern Link, c. 1921. The Colston Buildings are on the right.

AN EARLIER VIEW of the Worcester Road, Malvern Link.

COLSTON BUILDINGS, Malvern Link, in 1907. The corner shop is Galen House and is still a chemist. The side road on the right was then known as Church Terrace and is now Hampden Road.

WORCESTER ROAD, Malvern Link, during the 1920s. W.H. Smith & Son had a branch in Colston Buildings on the left until the early 1960s.

THE JUNCTION OF RICHMOND AND WORCESTER ROADS, Malvern Link, in 1929. Pembridge's the outfitters is now the site of Barclays Bank.

WORCESTER ROAD, Malvern Link, c. 1908. The Santler Motor Works can be seen on the right.

A VIEW OF MALVERN WELLS in 1906, from Stoneleigh on the left to St Peter's Church on the right.

THE JUNCTION OF WELLS AND HOLYWELL ROADS, c. 1900. The road on the left is now very busy in contrast with this tranquil scene.

Malvern Wells, Institute & Post Office.

MALVERN WELLS INSTITUTE and the adjoining Bishopstone, which at this time was the post office stores, run by F.M. Towndrow. Taken around 1908.

Malvern Wells.

LOOKING TOWARDS THE CHURCH INSTITUTE, Malvern Wells, c. 1910. The building on the right was a grocers.

A LITTLE CHANGED VIEW of Westminster Corner and St James' Church, West Malvern, dating from the early years of the century.

BROOMHILL, WEST MALVERN, c. 1910. The house on the right was used as apartments for many years and is now a hotel.

BARNARDS GREEN in 1904. Banham's has now been rebuilt, but the other two buildings still exist.

A VIEW OF BARNARDS GREEN in 1911 with Slack's Supply Stores on the right. The building is now hidden behind the façades of Dobsons and Robersons.

THE AVENUE, Newland, C. 1912, with the Worcester Road in the foreground.

Newland Almshouses, Malvern. Quadrangle S&E.

THE 3RD EARL BEAUCHAMP left money for the foundation of almshouses at Newland. They were built in 1862, added to in 1889 and 1900, and seen here C. 1920s.

THE WATER TANK in North Malvern Road around 1900. A clock tower was added in 1901.

THE GIRLS' FRIENDLY SOCIETY HOME just off the Wells Road. Used by them for over 40 years it is now flats.

POPLAR COTTAGE, Lower Howsell, home of Albert Lampitt, taken in 1914.

SECTION TWO

Around and About

MADRESFIELD VILLAGE and the parish church of St Mary the Virgin in a pre-First World War view.

THE VILLAGE PUMP, Madresfield, in 1953. The pump was opposite the post office and its position is now marked by the village notice board.

THE HOME OF THE LYGON FAMILY: this 1902 view of Madresfield Court shows it to be a fine example of a Tudor manor house.

A VISIT OF BIRMINGHAM DEAF AND DUMB INSTITUTE to Madresfield Court, c. 1890. Lord and Lady Beauchamp are seated third from the right and left respectively.

NURSE MAUD with Lord Elmley (later 8th Earl Beauchamp) and the Hon. Hugh Lygon (in pram) at Madresfield Court, c. 1906.

A GATHERING OF PEOPLE at Madresfield Court around 1919, including Viscount Elmley centre right.

A FÊTE at Madresfield Court held during the inter-war years.

MOTOR-CYCLE COMBINATION AND RIDER at a speed trial, Gloucester Drive, Madresfield Court, around 1921.

MADRESFIELD COURT STAFF on a picnic, c. 1908. Left to right: Mr Morgan, Miss Gillett, Mrs Aylett (the housekeeper), Miss Harris, Miss Cassidy(?), and Mrs Harper. The photograph was taken by another member of staff, Mr Love.

COLWALL STONE and post office, c. 1905.

THE PHOTOGRAPHER has the full attention of the dog on top of the Colwall stone. Taken in 1903.

AN EARLY TWENTIETH-CENTURY VIEW of Colwall with two Schweppes delivery vehicles.

AN ANONYMOUS GARDEN PARTY at Colwall, apparently prior to the First World War.

COLWALL BRASS BAND, c. 1906, with their conductor, George Alder, in the centre.

THE MALVERN HILLS from the Colwall Road, taken around 1910.

AN ALMOST COMPLETELY UNCHANGED Eastnor Post Office, pictured before the First World War.

AN EARLY VIEW of the Rectory House at Eastnor. The building has since been substantially altered and is now known as Eastnor Court.

MANY VIEWS OF EASTNOR CASTLE have been produced, but there are fewer pictures of the magnificent rooms inside. The top photograph is of the billiard room and the lower is of the sitting room. Both date from early in the century.

A PRE-FIRST WORLD WAR VIEW of the Wyche.

Malvern, The upper wyche

A VIEW OF THE UPPER WYCHE, little changed since the early part of the century.

LITTLE MALVERN PRIORY CHURCH and Court, around the late 1930s.

BLACKMORE PARK, home of the Hornyold family. The estate was broken up at auction in 1919 and the house was destroyed by fire shortly afterwards.

THE PLUME OF FEATHERS, Castlemorton (also known as the Feathers Inn). Taken in 1931.

CASTLEMORTON POST OFFICE during the 1920s. The Haigh family ran the business for over 20 years from around 1913.

CLIFFE'S ARMS, Mathon, c. 1900.

CRADLEY taken in 1926, a view virtually unchanged today.

STIFFORDS BRIDGE POST OFFICE and the Seven Stars Inn between 1910 and 1918, with an unknown band and parade.

ST JOHN THE BAPTIST CHURCH, Mathon, from the south-east. A view taken before the First World War.

WYNDS POINT, home of Jenny Lind, the Swedish Nightingale, from 1883 to 1887. This view was taken in 1907.

BRITISH CAMP HOTEL, Whitsun 1909, with a group on a cycling tour from Lancashire in the foreground.

BRITISH CAMP HOTEL and the Malvern Hills, 1931.

A VIEW OF THE BRITISH CAMP SWIMMING POOL during the late 1930s.

The Chace Lane, Upper Welland, Nr. Malvern

CHACE (OR CHASE) LANE. The lane off Upper Welland Road, now renamed Chase Road, is completely unrecognizable from this view of 1920.

Holy Trinity Choir, Welland - 1916.

HOLY TRINITY CHOIR, Welland, in 1916.

A GROUP IN FANCY DRESS on Guarlford Rectory lawn, c. 1914. The Revd Frederick Newsom, Rector of Guarlford, is on the far left.

LADIES VERSUS GENTLEMEN cricket teams at Guarlford, c. 1907.

CLEVELODE VILLAGE during the early years of the century.

THE HAYNES FAMILY outside the rear of their cottage in the main street of Bosbury. Almost unbelievably this photograph was taken as late as 1913.

AN EARLY VIEW OF CALLOW END. The buildings in the middle have disappeared.

CALLOW END POST OFFICE in 1915. The post office is now at the other end of the buildings and the original cottage has been extended.

A TIMELESS, but certainly pre-First World War, view of Hanley Castle.

QUAY LANE, Hanley Castle, c. 1923. The cross has now been moved and the building on the right has disappeared.

A VIEW OF T.A. TILT'S CREAMERY at Hanley Castle, C. 1920s. They supplied milk to the Malvern Dairy.

HANLEY SWAN POST OFFICE taken in 1954. At this time it was also a café.

SECTION THREE

The Hills

A STEREO PHOTOGRAPH of a group of donkey women, c. 1860s.

A HUMOROUS IMPRESSION from 1860 of water cure patients and others riding and walking up the hills.

DONKEY RIDERS on the Malvern Hills, c. 1918.

A GROUP WITH AN EARLY MOTOR CAR on the Worcestershire Beacon, c. 1900. Wheeled vehicles have been banned from the hills now for around 60 years.

THE TOPOSCOPE was installed at the top of the Worcestershire Beacon in 1897 to celebrate Queen Victoria's Jubilee. It shows landmarks which are visible on a clear day over a very wide area.

THE WORCESTERSHIRE BEACON CAFÉ, recently destroyed by fire, taken some time in the 1950s.

A GOLDEN JUBILEE BONFIRE on Worcestershire Beacon in 1887. The completed pyre rose 36 ft above the summit on a base 10 ft square.

NOW LARGELY OBSCURED BY FOLIAGE, this view was possible during the early years of the century from what was part of a panoramic walk above the town.

IVY SCAR ROCK was a popular subject for prints and photographs in Victorian and Edwardian times.

THE QUARRIES, North Malvern Road, with the clock tower in the middle distance, C. 1904.

A TRACTION ENGINE at Malvern Wells Quarry.

A LANDSLIP at the Wyche, c. 1915.

THE PROPOSED ROUTE for a chair lift, 1962. It was to start from Rose Bank Gardens and terminate 50 ft from the summit of Worcestershire Beacon.

WORCESTERSHIRE BEACON and hill paths, a popular view for Victorian and Edwardian photographers.

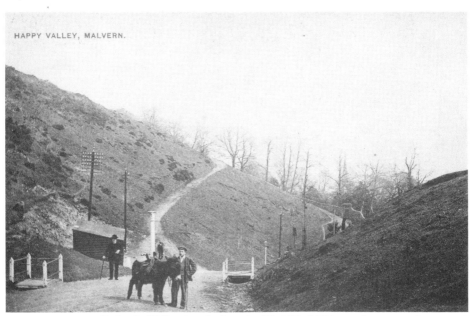

HAPPY VALLEY, near St Ann's Well, taken before the First World War and now much covered with trees.

EW FROM THE HEREFORDSHIRE BEACON, MALVERN.

A POPULAR VIEW from the Herefordshire Beacon. The reservoir was opened in 1895 to improve the water supply for the growing population of Malvern.

WEST MALVERN from Vinesend in 1915.

WEST MALVERN from the Birches, probably taken before the First World War.

Water and the Cure

DR JAMES MANBY GULLY (1808–82), the most famous of the water cure doctors. He arrived in Malvern in October 1842 and bought two houses on the Wells Road. His reputation in the 1870s was affected by the mysterious death of a patients' husband.

DR JAMES WILSON (1807–67) arrived in Malvern early in 1842 and built Priessnitz House in 1845. He was the first of the water cure doctors to arrive in Malvern.

Malvern.—The Tudor Hotel.

NEWBIE (LATER TUDOR) AND HOLYROOD HOUSES on the Wells Road bought by Dr Gully in 1842. From 1847 the two buildings were used to segregate the sexes! This early 1920s view shows its later use as a hotel.

THE GROUNDS OF TOWNSHEND HOUSE, Radnor (now College) Road, in 1861. Dr Ralph Grindrod had started his medical practice here ten years previously.

THIS WAS ORIGINALLY BUILT IN 1845 as Priessnitz House by Dr James Wilson. It was the first purpose-built water cure establishment in Malvern.

THE FRONT OF PRIESSNITZ HOUSE, C. 1940s. By this time the building was a hotel and had been extended.

ST ANN'S WELL in 1905. The original house was built early in the nineteenth-century and enlarged around 1860. Threatened with demolition in 1963, its future now seems safe.

THE WELL HOUSE at St Ann's Well with the attendant during the early years of the century. The pure water may still be drunk today.

THE STEPS TO ST ANN'S WELL REMAIN, but the buildings on the lower left have gone.

THE ROAD ON THE RIGHT still leads to St Ann's Well. This view was taken c. 1916.

'BLIND GEORGE' PULLEN played the harmonium at St Ann's Well virtually every day for over 50 years. For much of that time he walked about 4 miles from his home at Storridge, although in later years he lived in Malvern. Most postcards of St Ann's Well show 'Blind George' at work. He died in 1936.

BUILT IN 1843 at a cost of £400 the Holy Well has been restored in recent years. The canopy was removed during the 1930s. Water has been bottled here since 1622.

MALVERN WATERWORKS (now known as Bromsberrow Pumping Station) was built in 1905. It still supplies much of Malvern today.

People and Events

LADY EMILY FOLEY, the lady of the manor, in 1883. She was the daughter of the Duke of Montrose and married Edward Thomas Foley MP of Stoke Edith. She died in 1900, aged 94.

LADY LAMBERT laying the foundation stone of the new Public Library in Graham Road on 9 February 1905.

Malvern: The Free Library.

THE NEW PUBLIC LIBRARY as it appeared when opened in 1906.

THE ASSEMBLY ROOMS were built in 1884/5. The foundation stone was laid by Earl
Beauchamp on 26 July 1884 in the presence of Jenny Lind, Lady Emily Foley and other
notables. The construction was completed in less than a year and the premises opened on
1 July 1885, when this photograph was taken. The premises were extensively altered during
1927/8.

Malvern : The Hospital.

ORIGINALLY BUILT IN 1868, the hospital just off Newtown Road was replaced in 1911 by the existing hospital in Lansdowne Crescent. This view was taken c. 1905.

THE MATRON AND NURSES in the grounds of Newtown Road Hospital around 1905.

THE LAYING OF THE FOUNDATION STONE of Christchurch Memorial Hall and Parish Room, Barnards Green Road, May 1905, by Lady Yeatman-Biggs, wife of the Bishop of Worcester. The building is now used for auctions.

LORD ROBERTS opening a rifle range, pre-1914. The exact site is not known but it appears to have been at the rear of Belle Vue Terrace or Rose Bank.

SIR EDWARD ELGAR on his first Sunbeam bicycle on Guarlford Road, c. 1900. The bicycle was later given to August Jaeger, 'Nimrod' of the 'Enigma Variations'.

CRAEG LEA, MALVERN WELLS, home of Edward Elgar between 1899 and 1904.

GUSTAV HAMEL, the aviator, visited Malvern in 1912 or 1913. This view shows him taking off from Jamaica Meadow, Malvern Link.

GUSTAV HAMEL'S FLIGHT attracted large crowds.

MALVERN CYCLING CLUB outside the Hundred House, Great Witley, in 1890. From left to right: W.H. Stevens (grocer), C. Santler, -?-, F.W. Hayes (butcher), -?-, J. Need (Lygon Pharmacy), Stanley Baldwin (later prime minister), Mr Caldwell, Mr Foxwell, Mr Woods, Mr Sadler, H.K. Hogben, Mr Crudge, W. Santler, Mr Melhuish, Mr Gwynn and Mr Osborne.

WILLIAM CRUMP, the eminent Victorian horticulturist. For 36 years he was head gardener at Madresfield Court and founder of Madresfield Agricultural Society. He died in 1932, aged 89. For some years he lived in Richmond Road.

RICHMOND ROAD, Malvern Link, looking towards Worcester Road, c. 1920s. William Crump lived at Oakridge, the second house from the right. The house has recently been refurbished.

JENNY LIND, the Swedish Nightingale, one of the greatest nineteenth-century singers. She lived at Wynds Point, next to the British Camp Hotel, from 1883 to 1887. This photograph was taken c. 1880.

MORGAN MOTORS FOOTBALL CLUB 1920/1, taken at the Royal Oak, Worcester Road. H.F.S. Morgan and A. Hales (works manager) are seated far right and left respectively.

GUARLFORD FOOTBALL CLUB 1919/20. The Revd Frederick Newsom, Rector of Guarlford, is second from left in the back row.

MALVERN FIRE BRIGADE C. 1890s – note the dog. The main fire station was in Victoria Road with another in Malvern Wells.

A FIRE AT HOPE END, Colwall, 1910.

LIEUT. H. KEEN of Malvern Fire Brigade. He was injured while on duty at a rick fire at Blackmore and died in Malvern Hospital on 21 August 1916.

GPO STAFF outside the post office in 1907. The ivy-covered building is the old vicarage, now part of the enlarged modern post office.

AN UNIDENTIFIED PARADE moving up Church Street in 1911.

NEWLAND AND MADRESFIELD SCOUT GROUP during the late 1930s.

THE FUNERAL OF GILBERT GORDON LEWIS (aged 31) of Redland Road in 1933. He was Superintendent of the St John's Ambulance, South Worcestershire Corps.

LORD ROBERT AND LADY BADEN-POWELL at the Guides and Scouts World Jamboree, Eastnor Park, May 1937.

A HUNT MEET on the Worcester Road during the inter-war years. The White Horse Hotel is now an estate agent's office and the Malvern Dairy is now a chinese restaurant.

THE HUNT IN WEST MALVERN, with St James' Church on the right, taken in the 1950s.

DAY TRIPPERS FROM BIRMINGHAM on Malvern Link Common on a bank holiday in 1907. Part of Strickland's Fair is on the right.

STRICKLAND'S FAIR, Link Common, c. 1900. Mr Strickland ran the fairs here until 1914.

STRICKLAND'S FAIR, 1905.

A GOSPEL MEETING at Malvern during the First World War.

MISS KATE WOODWARD, the winner of a decorated cycle parade in Malvern Link in 1913.

THE MALVERN LINK decorated cycle parade in 1913, with the winner, Kate Woodward, in front.

THE RED CROSS CARNIVAL, Malvern Link, 1915. In the background Gedge the Chemists can be seen on the corner of the Church Terrace (now Hampden Road).

A DECORATED CYCLE PARADE at Malvern Link Carnival, c. 1912.

CLEM WALTON was a barber, photographer and bookies' runner, who had a little shop in Court Road, Barnards Green. Despite the fact that he had only one eye he was one of the best photographic chroniclers of the area. This photograph was taken in the mid-1930s and shows a clock presented to him by Malvern Link Men's Own Brotherhood.

CLEM WALTON photographed many local school groups over the years. The girls here are from Malvern Girls' College in the 1940s.

THE MALVERN AMATEUR DRAMATIC CLUB was founded in 1869 at the Drill Hall, Albert Road. In 1874 the club moved to the Concert Hall in Church Street (Cecelia Hall), but reverted to the Drill Hall in 1879. This latter move was not popular with the public and a final move was made in July 1885 to the newly opened Assembly Rooms. This photograph of c. 1875/6 was apparently taken in Cecelia Hall. The second and third from the left are J.A. Walker (actor-manager) and Tom Webster. The second from the right is F.G. Russell.

MALVERN FESTIVAL cast and production staff in 1936. If you look closely you will see Stewart Granger (then known as James Stewart), his wife Elspeth March, Wendy Hiller, Ernest Thesiger and a number of other familiar faces of the period.

LINK PIERROTS, 1914.

H.C. BURGESS AND HIS ORCHESTRA in the Priory Park bandstand during the 1939 Malvern Festival.

Wm Towndrow, 1892

WILLIAM TOWNDROW'S grocery and drapery business was started in Malvern Link in 1831. He retired in 1874 but later became agent for the Worcester City & County Bank. He died in 1896, four years after this photograph was taken.

A RAGS, BOTTLES AND BONES DEALER, of unknown name, from the Belmont district of Malvern. Probably taken at the Hawthorn Inn, Upper Welland.

AN OX ROAST at North Malvern, apparently organized by Ebenezer Smith, a butcher of Newtown Road, prior to 1916.

TOBOGGANING at Malvern — a spill!

BIRMINGHAM MOTOR-CYCLE CAR RALLY on Malvern Link Common, March 1914.

RED HILL, Malvern Link Common, c. 1905.

A PICNIC on Wells Common, c. 1923.

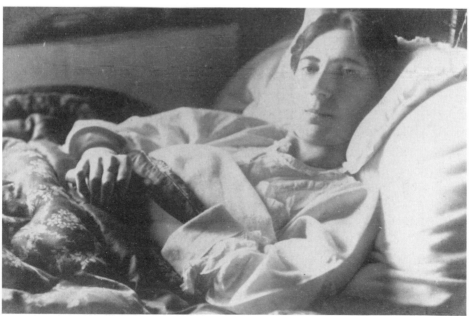

MRS FOLEY HOBBS after whom the famous white rose was named in 1910. This photograph was taken in 1917, apparently in Barnards Green. She died in 1920.

A DRIVE AFTER A WEDDING BREAKFAST at Newland in 1911.

BANK STREET BRETHREN Sunday School outing in 1906.

SECTION SIX

War and Peace

THE 11TH COMPANY, SECOND BATTALION WORCESTER RIFLE VOLUNTEERS encampment at Malvern, 11 August 1866. Thomas Cox of Cox & Painter (now Warwick House) is sitting in the tent entrance.

SIR HARRY VERNON and officers of the 11th Company Second Battalion Worcester Rifle Volunteers at Malvern in August 1866.

THE RIFLE VOLUNTEERS BAND at encampment, August 1866.

DAVID LLOYD GEORGE at the camp of the 13th Pioneer Battalion of the Glosters at Malvern on 13 June 1915.

THE 16TH SERVICE BATTALION ROYAL WARWICKSHIRE REGIMENT camp at Malvern during the First World War.

VOLUNTEERS PARADING in Malvern Link, 1914.

THE QUEEN'S OWN HUSSARS on Malvern Link Common, probably during the First World War.

THE FUNERAL OF DRIVER THOMAS WILLIAM PANTING, Royal Field Artillery, in 1917 at Guarlford Church. He died aged 20.

THE RED CROSS used the old hospital in Newtown during the First World War. It was staffed by members of the Voluntary Aid Detachment, seen here with some of the patients.

STAFF OF A MALVERN CONVALESCENT HOME in 1919.

CELEBRATING THE END OF THE WAR with Germany, May 1945 (VE Day), in Pound Bank Road.

ANOTHER VE DAY GROUP in Pound Bank Road.

Education, Commerce, Industry and Transport

Malvern—The College, Chapel and Pavilion.

MALVERN BOYS' COLLEGE was opened in 1865. This photograph dates from around 1904.

AN INSIDE VIEW of Malvern Boys' College, probably from the 1920s. Notice the sports trophies.

MALVERN GIRLS' COLLEGE, probably around the early 1920s. The original 'steeple' of the Imperial Hotel was removed soon after its purchase by the college. A further section of the tower has since been removed.

THE INTERIOR OF A SITTING ROOM in Malvern Girls' College, *c.* 1920.

MISS SMITH'S SCHOOL, The Manse, Malvern Wells, C. 1904. The house has since been converted into individual units.

THE ABBEY SCHOOL, Malvern Wells, hard courts, C. 1920s.

LAWNSIDE SCHOOL in Albert Road (South). Taken at the rear of the building overlooking the lawns, c. 1890s.

THE HAZEL BANK GIRLS' SCHOOL existed from around 1876 to 1907. This photograph dates from the 1890/95 period. The school building, on the Worcester Road, is now occupied by part of Hillside School.

CLARENDON SCHOOL, Cowleigh Road; its pupils going for a picnic in 1907. Miss Amy Flint, the headmistress from the opening of the school in 1898 until she retired in 1930, is on the extreme right in the back row of the coach. The school moved to Wales in 1948.

CLARENDON SCHOOL JUNIORS in class with Miss Calthrop, c. 1908. She joined the school in 1907 and remained for ten years.

THE EMPEROR HAILE SELASSIE OF ABYSSINIA in Malvern, c. 1939, to visit his grandchildren at Clarendon School. During his visit he attended the school prize giving and concert at the Winter Gardens.

E. GRIMLEY, SCOTLAND HOUSE, Cowleigh Road, were general drapers and outfitters from around 1902 to 1915. Since then the building has been a motor showroom and engineers.

H. BRAY & CO, tailors and outfitters, as they were c. 1918. This part of the Worcester Road was then known as the Promenade.

MALVERN LINK CO-OPERATIVE SOCIETY, Upper Welland. The shop, almost next to the Hawthorn Inn, was in existence from 1905 to c. 1913. It has since been demolished.

ARCHIBALD JONES delivering eggs in Alexandra Road, c. 1924.

C. SPENCER, BUTCHERS, Court Road, Barnards Green, 1920.

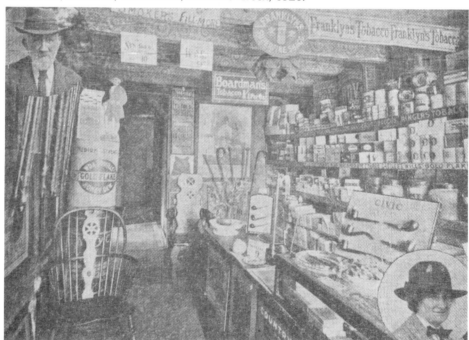

THE INSIDE OF 'YE OLDE BACCY SHOPPE', Claremont Cottage, Malvern Link, in 1928. Run by the Fillmore family for over 70 years, it was demolished in 1963 and is now the site of a bank.

J.N. HOLMES, LEIGH COURT DAIRY, milk float, c. 1907. The firm delivered in Malvern twice daily.

T.A. TILT & SON'S milk delivery vehicle at the Hanley Castle Creamery.

ONE OF ABSALOM BRADSHAW'S milk delivery carts from Guarlford Court. The photograph was taken on the Link Common during the late 1890s.

BUCHANAN HOUSE, Church Street, 1871, now the site of Woolworths. Wm. Sparkes were furnishing ironmongers, cutlers, gas fitters, lamp and oil dealers, braziers, bath manufacturers, etc!

THE WHITE HORSE HOTEL, Worcester Road, is now used as an estate agents. Herbert Jones was the licensee for ten years from around 1912.

DAVID KENDALL opened a draper's shop in Church Street in 1852, moving to a shop adjoining the Beauchamp (later the Royal Malvern) Hotel in 1854. This photograph was taken in 1910.

J. COLEY & SON, Church Street, c. 1907, cycle and motor depot and suppliers of sports equipment, gramophones, records, etc! The building is now part of Church Walk.

NURSE THE GROCERS, Belmont Place, Malvern Wells, in the nineteenth century. The business continued until recent times.

THE ROYAL WELL BREWERY in West Malvern Road in the early years of the century. In the background is the Concert Hall, built with seating for 2,000 in 1883. The hall closed in 1895 and was demolished during the late 1930s.

E. GILLETT BURTON'S REMOVAL VAN, *c.* 1930s. Gillett Burton is on the left and Archibald Jones is by the door. The business was based at Guarlford.

E. GILLETT BURTON'S GUARLFORD TAXI during the 1930s. Archibald Jones is at the wheel.

F.S. RANFORD, Barnards Green, sales and servicing vehicle around 1903.

THE INTERIOR OF F.S. Ranford's garage, c. 1914. AB 79 is a 10 hp Swift.

THE MORGAN FACTORY, Worcester Road, November 1913, with motor-cycle show cars. Now the site of Brooklyn Garage.

THE MORGAN CAR COMPANY despatch bay, Pickersleigh Road, 1928.

THE INSIDE OF H.E.J. Morgan's garage, Worcester Road, 1907, two years before the first 'Morgan' was built.

MACHINES OUTSIDE C. Santler & Co., Northumberland Works, Howsell Road, Malvern Link, c. 1898. The date 1837 for the boneshaker is wildly out – 1868 would be more reasonable.

THE QUEST HILLS ROAD, Malvern Link, workshop of Santler Bros, pioneers in cycle-building in the area. Two high-wheeled 'ordinaries' and a tricycle can be seen here in the mid-1880s.

A 6 HP SANTLER CAR built c. 1901, registered AB 171 in January 1904, seen here outside the Northumberland Works, Howsell Road. T.C. Santler is at the wheel and W.R. Santler is seated in front. All the staff of the business are present in this photograph. It is now known that the Santlers produced the first four-wheeled internal combustion motor car in Britain in 1889.

THE HEREFORDSHIRE AND WORCESTERSHIRE AGRICULTURAL SHOW opening ceremony of 1905. The event was apparently held on a site off Court Road.

THE MADRESFIELD AGRICULTURAL SHOW before the First World War.

OSIER (WILLOW) CUTTERS between Guarlford and Clevelode in the 1920s.

HOP PICKERS AT LEIGH SINTON before the First World War. There were several hop growers in the area at the time.

A HORSE TEAM at Bullocks Farm, Guarlford, c. 1890s. Left to right: John Hadley, William Bullock and an unidentified boy.

GREAT MALVERN RAILWAY STATION in 1861.

GIPSY LASS, built *c.* 1840, at Great Malvern station in 1861.

MALVERN LINK STATION, the 'down' platform and building, c. 1861.

COLWALL TUNNEL CUTTING and north portal during its construction, c. 1860.

Colwall Railway Station.

This is the place where Grandmother lives — two stations from Malvern ... over from Aef.

COLWALL RAILWAY STATION 1907.

GREAT MALVERN STATION some time between the wars.

A TRAIN PASSING through Malvern Link station, 1905.

A DERAILED ENGINE at Malvern Wells, December 1957.

MALVERN WELLS, HANLEY ROAD STATION on the Malvern–Tewkesbury line in 1957, showing the disused overgrown station and line.

THE OLD UPTON TO MALVERN RAILWAY LINE BRIDGE near Welland about to be blown up by Ron Gamstone in March 1970.

ACKNOWLEDGEMENTS

I would like to express my sincere thanks to all those who have helped me to compile this collection of photographs. The staff of Malvern Library and the County Record Offices have been unfailingly patient and have allowed me to use many photographs in their collections. Other people who have helped me and lent photographs are as follows:

J. Alderton • A. Ballard • *Berrows Journal* • Miss J. Bradshaw • R.J. Collins
Demaus Transport Photographics • Miss D. Drake • Miss A. Flint
Miss E. Hawker • Mr & Mrs A. Jones • Malvern Fire Station • *Malvern Gazette*
D. Massey • Mrs E. Oseman • J. Passey • D. Postle • Mrs V.A. Powell
Mrs J. Preece • K. Rickards • Mrs J. Roberts • A. Russell • R.H. Sargeant
C.H. Spencer • H. Stanley • A.J. Webb • *Worcester Evening News*

My thanks also go to all those who have answered my numerous questions, and to my wife who has put up with more than she will admit.

Every effort has been made to ascertain photographic copyright where appropriate.